M. POSSIBLE

F. Darnell Bateman

AuthorHouse™
1663 Liberty Drive
Bloomington, IN 47403
www.authorhouse.com
Phone: 833-262-8899

Because of the dynamic nature of the Internet, any web addresses or links contained in this book may have changed since publication and may no longer be valid. The views expressed in this work are solely those of the author and do not necessarily reflect the views of the publisher, and the publisher hereby disclaims any responsibility for them.

This book is printed on acid-free paper.

ISBN: 978-1-6655-1668-6 (sc)
ISBN: 978-1-6655-1674-7 (hc)
ISBN: 978-1-6655-1673-0 (e)

Library of Congress Control Number: 2021902772

Print information available on the last page.

Published by AuthorHouse 02/11/2021

authorHOUSE

It is possible to be the best at whatever I do.

I can run faster.

I can jump higher.

I can be smarter.

Even if no one
believes I can be.

It is possible to be the best at whatever I do.

I can draw better.

I can color prettier.

I can paint more brilliant.

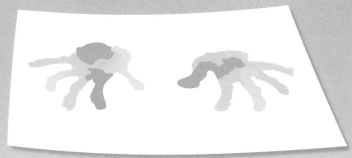

Than anyone believes I can.

I can love more.

I can do so many things.

I can dream...

Of anything I want to do.

I can be a great leader...

Or a great follower,

Simply because
I want to be.

It is possible to be whatever I choose and do whatever I dream.

I am M. Possible because I do the things others don't think I can do.

Are you M. Possible too?

What can you do?

Printed in the United States
By Bookmasters